NATIONAL GEOGRAPHIC

Making a Hat

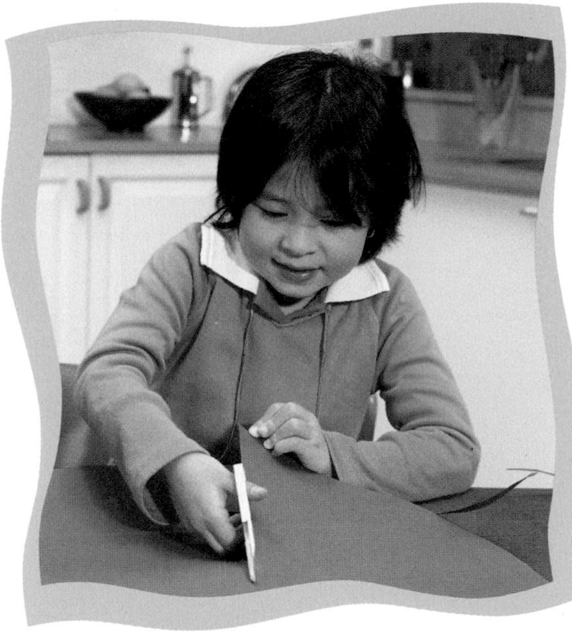

Kate McGough

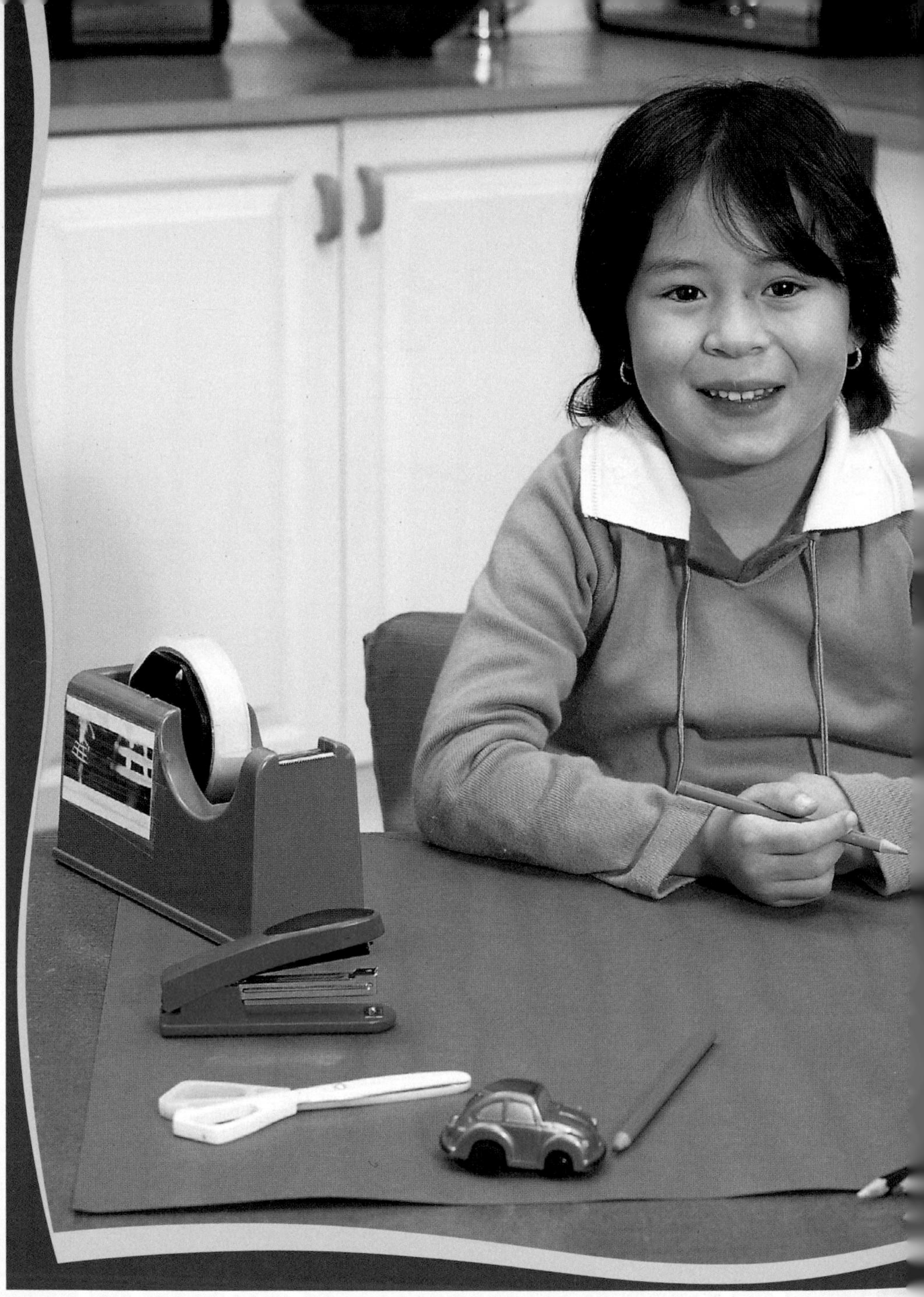

I can make a hat.

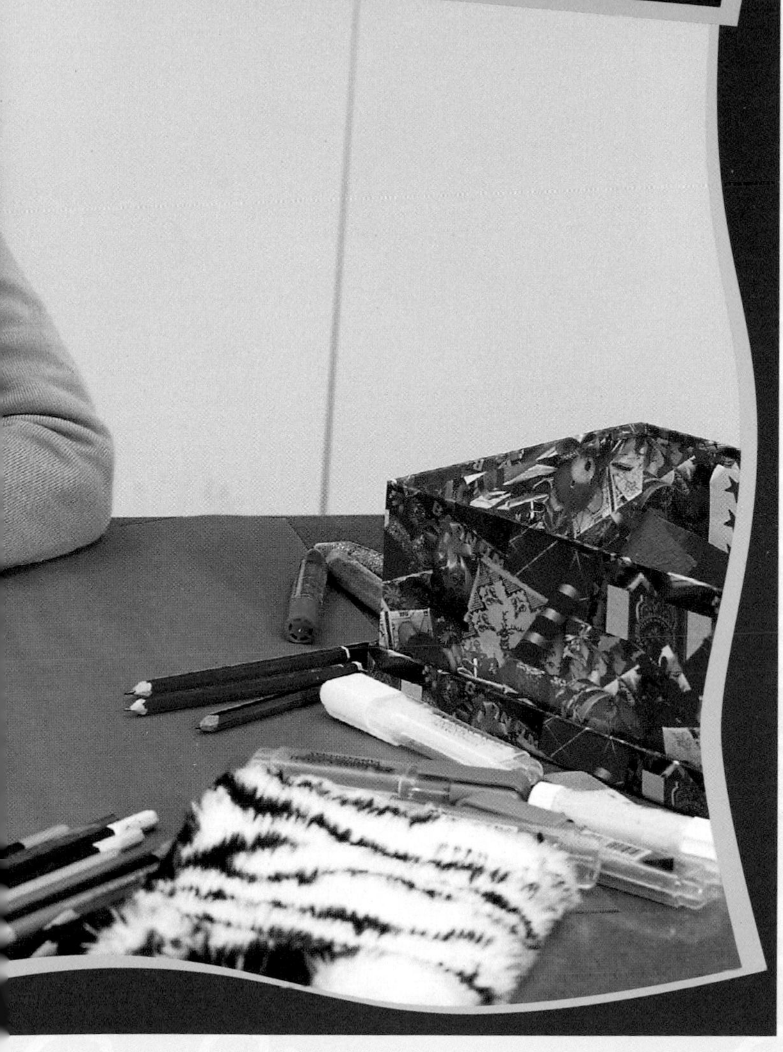

I use scissors.

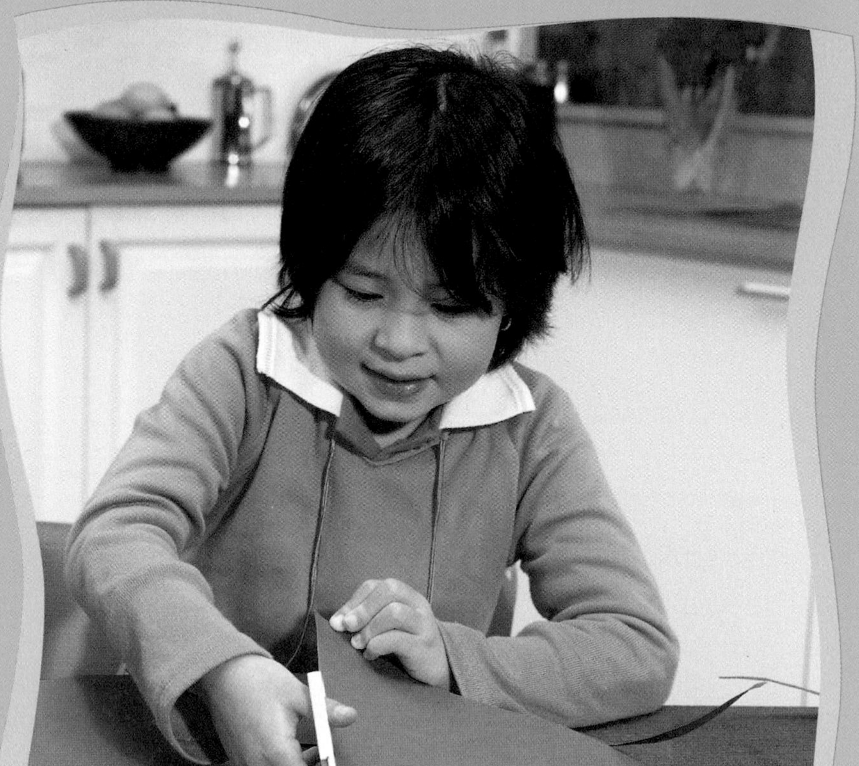

I use a stapler.

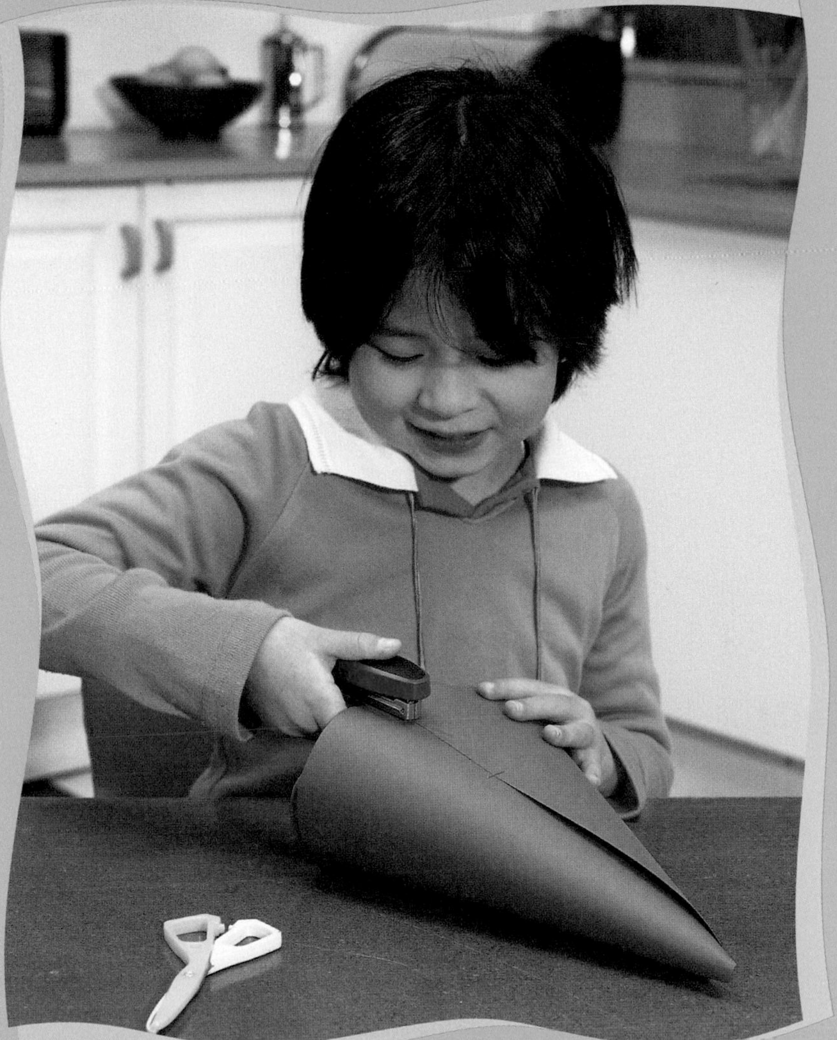

I use colored pencils.

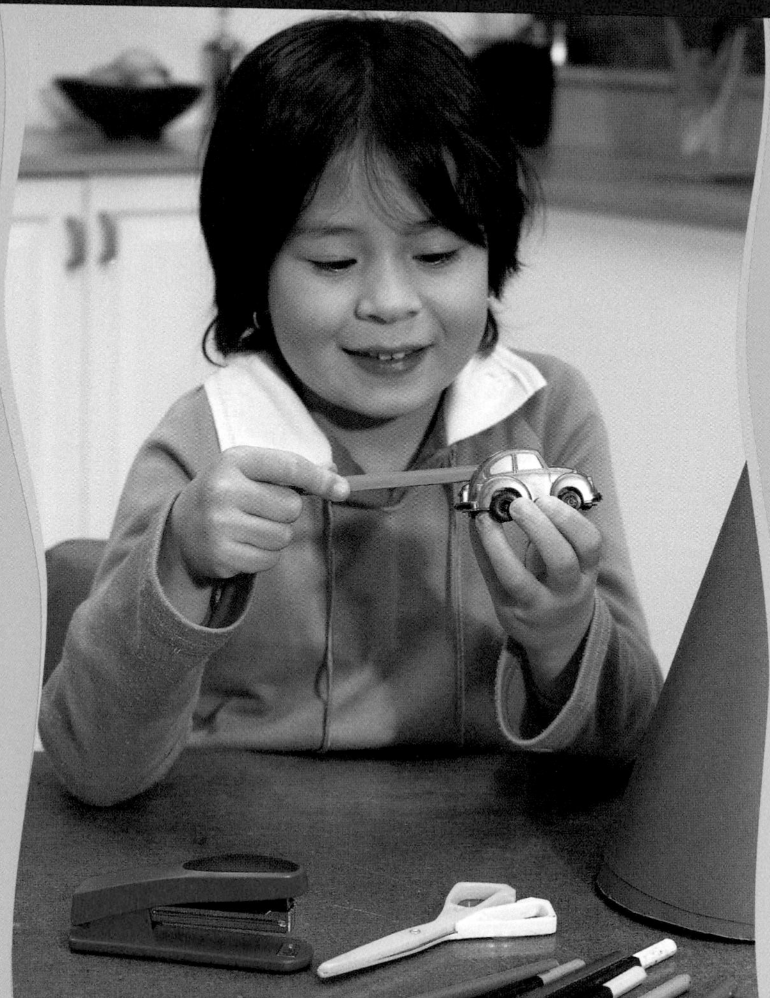

I use tape.

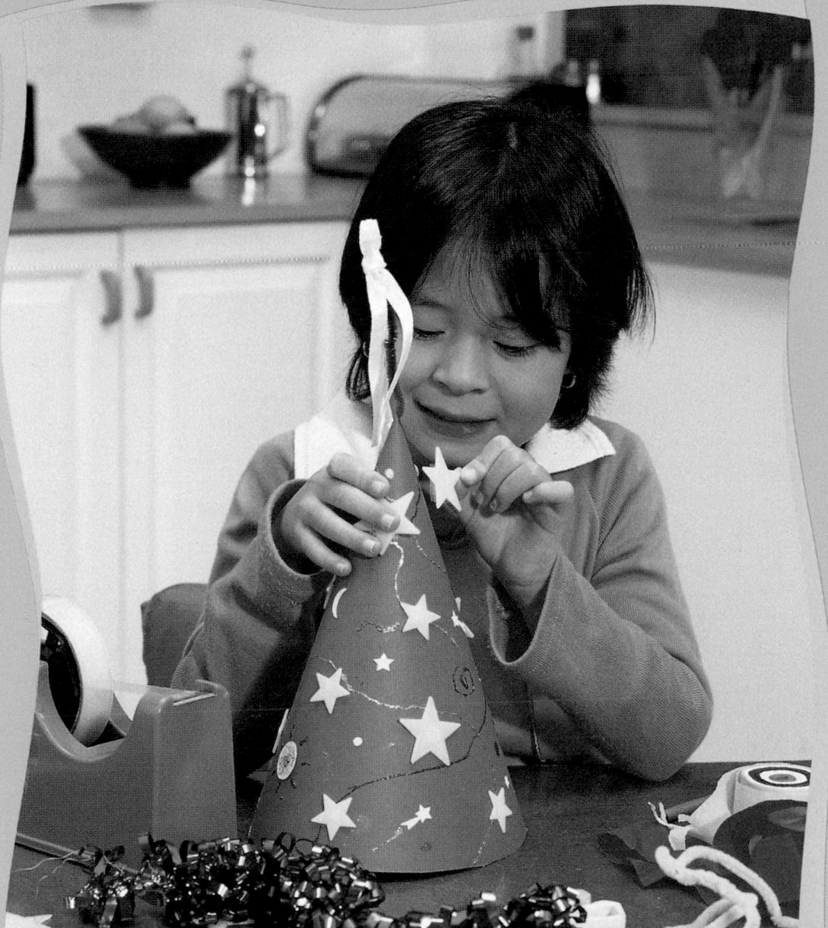

I can wear my hat!

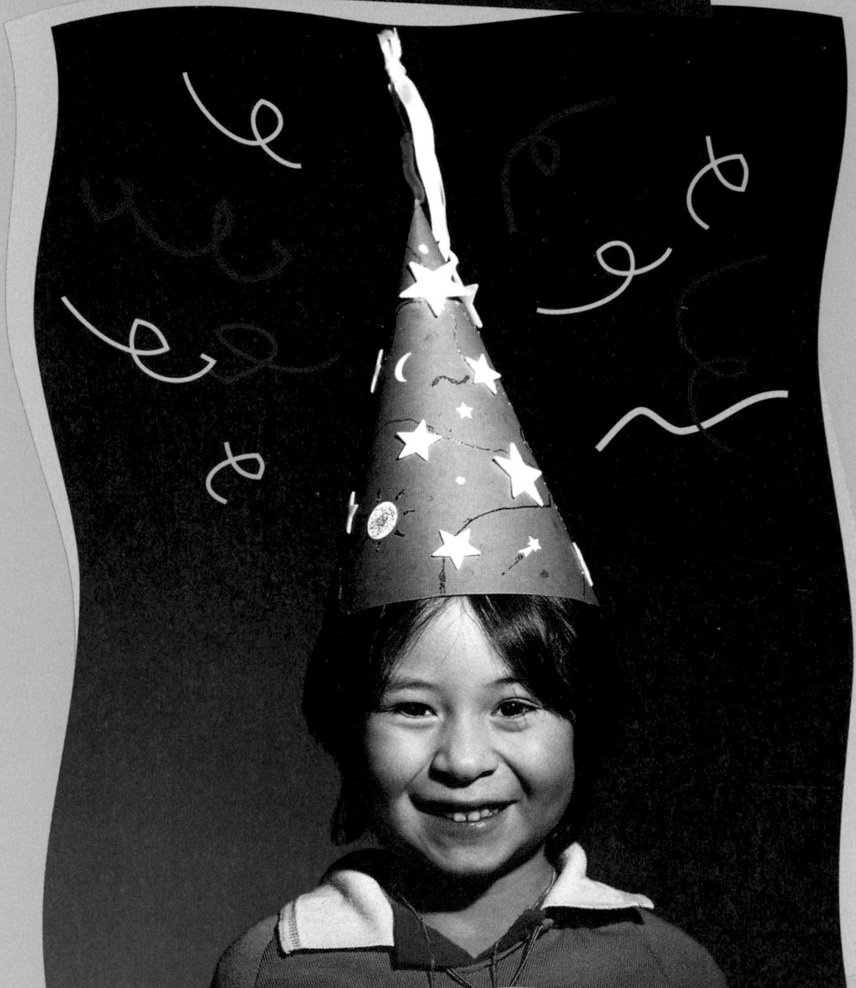